love 2 Diane from Brenda SEPT.26. 2006

C000134034

The Inner Beauty Series
Defining Your Worth in the Eyes of God

LOOK
Beyond
WHAT YOU SEE

Charisma
HOUSE
Books about Spirit-Led Living

Lisa Bevere

Look Beyond What You See by Lisa Bevere
Published by Charisma House
A part of Strang Communications Company
600 Rinehart Road
Lake Mary, Florida 32746
www.charismahouse.com

Cover design by Rachel Campbell

Library of Congress Catalog Card Number: 2001099921
International Standard Book Number: 0-88419-841-3

02 03 04 05   87654321
Printed in the United States of America

Contents

Introduction

I n this third book in the Inner Beauty Series, we are going to take a closer look at where real beauty can be found—and some of the things that keep real beauty from being seen.

As a human, you are created in the image of God, and there are multiple dimensions of you.

> Then God said, "Let us make man in our image, in our likeness…" So God created man in his own image, in the image of God he created him; male and female he created them.
>
> —Genesis 1:26–27

To understand—and develop—the real beauty God created you to show, you must understand each of these dimensions of body, soul and spirit.

First, there is the physical or natural dimension of you. It is what you see when you look in the mirror. It is the image reflected and projected to others. It functions in conjunction with the five senses. It sees, smells, tastes, hears and touches. It is the outer shell that houses you. It protects, nourishes, grows, reproduces, ages and eventually dies.

> ## Our physical body in itself is a testament to the glory of God.

This physical realm can be broken, scarred, wounded, healed and strengthened. To some degree it can be altered, but physically each of us is the product of a genetic compilation passed down through centuries of reproduction. Our physical bodies are not unlike fruit trees, which grow from seed form to full maturity. We pass through stages of growth and harvest, each varying in their timing and season.

Our physical body in itself is a testament to the glory of God. In all of man's years of study it is still a mystery. Man cannot create; he can only clone, or re-create, human life. We cannot *produce* life; we merely *reproduce*. A creator originates, not duplicates. God is the *Creator* of all life. He is the Creator of your individual life and physical form. He was intimately involved in each detail. Surely you have witnessed the miracle and wonder of a baby. It is the very handiwork of God.

> You knit me together in my mother's womb. I praise you because I am fearfully and wonderfully made; your works are wonderful, I know that full well.
> —PSALM 139:13–14

We can all look at a baby and see the miracle, but can you look at your self today and say the same? Can you call your self fearfully and wonderfully made? Or is the wonder crowded out by a list of shortcomings and flaws? Don't answer me; I already know your answer.

Your physical self, though the most obvious, is the least representative of the real you. The physical can only touch physically. You cannot physically reach within your self and touch your soul. That is the real you.

Though you cannot touch it and though you've never seen it, you know your soul is there. The soul has a range of emotional senses all its own. It is the part of you that feels—not physically but emotionally. In your soul you experience happiness, sadness, joy and pain. If you were ever made fun of, it was your soul—not your physical body—that experienced the pain.

The soul consists of your mind, will and emotions. It is the place of expression of your person—your personality. It houses your thoughts, your hopes, your dreams and your fears. Though the physical cannot reach in and physically touch the soul, your soul is nourished by physical affection as well as wounded by physical abuse. A hug can spill over from the physical and warm your soul. A slap can sting your heart as well as your face. Your soul lives in your body. It can exercise power over your physical body.

In times of danger, the soul can override the body's physical capacity. We have all heard stories of great feats of strength where will has overcome matter, where the human desire is so great it supersedes physical odds. This can be found with athletes or with a parent whose child is in danger. There are also accounts of those who have been paralyzed by fear—physically capable yet frozen by sheer will power.

The soul can imprint itself on us outwardly. Fear, grief or anger can etch themselves upon a face after years of expressing physically the inner turmoil of the soul. Likewise, joy, peace and strength can leave their mark on a face. Fear of rejection can change a person's posture, causing one to cower or stoop, while confidence holds another erect and straight.

Just as our physical bodies were created by God, so is the soul.

> For you created my inmost being…
> —Psalm 139:13

The soul is the inner being. It should be governed by the will, which is governed by our strongest base of influence. It draws information from our mind and considers our physical needs in its analysis of natural information. It draws on past experiences and is forged and molded with each passing day. It can be both analytical and emotional. The soul is different from the physical body, yet the soul inhabits the body much as a hand fills a glove. The body is lifeless, expressionless and useless without the soul.

A third dimension is the spirit, which is often described as your heart.

> Love the Lord your God with all your heart and with all your soul and with all your mind and with all your strength.
> —Mark 12:30

This scripture lists these different avenues of expression in order of their preeminence:

1. Our heart or spirit
2. Our soul
3. Our mind and strength

When our lives are divinely ordered, our spirit will direct our soul and mind, which in turn will guide our physical self. It is the goal of this book to introduce truths to you that will lead you into a proper restoration of all of these areas. If you are ready for transformation, "then you will know the truth, and the truth will set you free" (John 8:32).

When our lives are divinely
ordered, our spirit will
direct our soul and mind,
which in turn will guide
our physical self.

As you experience the transformation power of
God to see beyond what you have seen before, you
will move from that worldly, false mirror image by
which you have identified yourself in the past. You
will begin to see the real beauty you possess
within, and you will learn to radiate that beauty to
all the people whom you encounter.

Read on, and discover your real beauty!

Adapted from Lisa Bevere, *You Are Not What You Weigh*,
7–10.

Inner Beauty Tip

The real you
is not the image
reflected in
your mirror.

You Are Not
What You See

The LORD does not look at the things man
looks at. Man looks at the outward appearance, but the LORD looks at the heart.

—1 SAMUEL 16:7

hen you look in your mirror, what do you see?
Chances are, like most women, you can com-
pile an immediate list of shortcomings, flaws
and wrinkles punctuated by a couple of assets. Your
natural assessment may be correct, but you need to
know something: What you see is not who you are.

You are someone no one sees—not your husband, your friends or even your parents. The real
you is invisible to the scrutiny of the natural eye

and often misrepresented by your outward actions. The real you is not the image greeting you in the mirror. Our outward image can never accurately reflect our inward nature. Our true life is hidden.

One day while critically assessing my reflection I heard the Holy Spirit ask, "What do you see?"

I promptly answered, "A tired, stressed mother."

He gently reminded me, "You are not what you see."

I immediately argued, looking closer in the mirror, "I am tired, and I am stressed, and I do look it!"

Again I heard, "You are not what you see."

True, I felt tired and stressed, but that was not who I was—it was what I felt. My reflection was true, but it was not the truth. My feelings and conditions are subject to change while God's truth remains unchanged and anchored in His Word. I am spirit, not body. I have a body, but I am not a body. I was assessing myself by what I had, not by who I was.

"You are not what you see."

A Revealing Position

Earlier in my life I enjoyed a unique career as a promotional representative for a top cosmetic line. I was also a television makeup artist on the weekends. Representing the cosmetic line, I traveled an eight-state territory. Nearly every Monday morning I boarded a plane to visit a new city. I would do makeovers on women all week and return to Dallas on Friday afternoon. It was wonderful. I stayed in the finest hotels, enjoyed room service, a bubble bath and about three hours of Bible reading nightly. Best of all, my days were spent making woman feel better about themselves.

I had always enjoyed playing with makeup, but beyond that, I had developed it as a talent in order to hide my own flaws. I lost my right eye to cancer at the age of five, and the size and shape of my artificial eye differed from that of my real eye. Therefore, I played with makeup in my teen years to make both eyes appear to be the same. Now I could use the talent I developed to benefit others.

What intrigued me the most, however, had nothing to do with applying makeup—it was what happened when I removed the makeup of the woman on whom I was working.

Women came to the counter confidently to check in for their appointments. They asked a few questions, looked at the last woman I worked on and studied the available products and colors.

As I worked on each new client I put up a privacy screen or took the woman to a private room. As I cleansed her face, I could almost see each woman cower and glance warily around—even if we were alone. Apologies were made for untweezed eyebrows and imperfections of her skin. Many seemed fearful and anxious. They wanted me to know that they did not look this way.

I reassured each woman she was beautiful by quickly pointing out her assets. "You have beautiful eyes," or "What a great lip line." As the makeup went back on, each woman's confidence returned layer by layer. She felt safe again, asking me questions like, "How did you do that?" or "Where do I stop my liner?" Soon we were the best of friends.

Women often apologized for being so nervous, bought a large supply of makeup and skin care products and left with renewed confidence.

It pleased me when a client left happy, but I was nevertheless disturbed that a woman would feel so vulnerable and unattractive without her makeup. It was almost as if I had uncovered something she was ashamed of, something she felt she should hide—her face.

Who Sets the Standard?

Perhaps you feel the same way. You may defend your position by reasoning that all women feel this way! This may be true—but should they? You are not what you see!

We have compared ourselves to a standard of perfection—one that always finds us wanting. It is the standard we find in the checkout line in the grocery store as we glance at the women on the covers of the fashion or fitness magazines. It is the one manufactured (and I do mean manufactured) by Hollywood. It is the standard set by those who labor for that which perishes. Their entire lives are centered on maintaining an image or an appearance.

By this standard, youth and folly are exalted while age and wisdom are despised. This is expected in the world, but I am not addressing the world right now. I'm talking to the church. We have allowed the world to set the pace and direct our taste. The world's system measures from the outside in while God measures from the inside out. The world loves appearances and hates the truth. God loves the truth and hates deceptive appearances.

> The world's system measures from the outside in while God measures from the inside out.

Living Under the Influence

The women of Israel had come under the influence of the culture of their day. They allowed the culture around them to dictate the measure of a woman. They adorned themselves in the manner of the Gentiles, with each accessory designed to draw attention to them.

Moreover, the Lord said, Because the

> daughters of Zion are haughty and walk
> with outstretched necks and with undisci-
> plined (flirtatious and alluring) eyes, trip-
> ping along with mincing and affected gait,
> and making a tinkling noise with [the
> anklets on] their feet, therefore the Lord
> will smite with a scab the crown of the
> heads of the daughters of Zion [making
> them bald], and the Lord will cause them to
> be [taken as captives and to suffer the
> indignity of being] stripped naked. In that
> day the Lord will take away the finery.
> —Isaiah 3:16–18, AMP

Isaiah continued to describe in detail all the fin-
ery that would be stripped away, everything from
jewelry to hand mirrors, robes to undergarments,
headbands to handbags. Sound familiar? Then he
concluded:

> And it shall come to pass that instead of the
> sweet odor of spices there shall be the
> stench of rottenness; and instead of a gir-
> dle, a rope; and instead of well-set hair,
> baldness; and instead of a rich robe, a gird-
> ing of sackcloth; and searing [of captives by

the scorching heat] instead of beauty.
—Isaiah 3:24, amp

Eventually the influence of their culture led the Israelites into bondage and captivity. They lost all the beauty they had taken such pains to create and all the accessories they had used to accent it.

Camel Queens

These women were a far cry from Rebekah who was drawing water from a well when she won a beauty contest and her prince.

> And the girl was very beautiful and attractive, chaste and modest, and unmarried. And she went down to the well, filled her water jar, and came up.
> —Genesis 24:16, amp

Rebekah was not adorned with costly apparel that drew attention to herself. How glamorous do you doll up for fetching water in the desert? She was adorned with good works. She was busy serving her family, and when she met a stranger she extended him hospitality.

After she had given him a drink, she said,

8

"I'll draw water for your camels too, until they have finished drinking." So she quickly emptied her jar into the trough, ran back to the well to draw more water, and drew enough for all his camels. Without saying a word, the man watched her closely to learn whether or not the Lord had made his journey successful. When the camels had finished drinking, the man took out a gold nose ring weighing a beka and two gold bracelets weighing ten shekels.

—Genesis 24:19–22

Her service won her adornment. She had not labored for the ring or bracelets. She had no idea these would be given to her. She labored because she was a servant.

Likewise, our good works bring us adornment as well as God's provision. It is interesting to note that Rebekah was given some of the same things that were later snatched away from the daughters of Zion. Jewelry was not the issue. Motive was. The daughters of Zion were too proud to serve. They spent their strength and wealth adorning and serving themselves instead of serving others. When calamity hit they were left without covering or provision.

God is not telling us to throw away our makeup and jewelry. I wear makeup and jewelry, but it is not what I labor for. The important thing is how you spend your strength and how you measure your worth. What do you allow to influence your life?

> Do you adorn the hidden with the same zeal as you adorn the outward? If we are honest, most of us will admit we do not. We dress up our outward selves to the neglect of the inward. Others dress their outward to conceal their inward condition:
>
> You say, "I am rich; I have acquired wealth and do not need a thing." But you do not realize that you are wretched, pitiful, poor, blind and naked.
>
> —REVELATION 3:17

Untangle yourselves from the superficial and embrace the supernatural.

We need to stop trying to conceal our inward conditions and instead allow God to heal us. He already knows our true conditions, yet He loves us. Untangle yourselves from the superficial and embrace the supernatural. It is urgent that we consecrate and separate ourselves, not by rending natural garments, but by tearing the hidden veil from our hearts.

> Rend your heart
> and not your garments.
> Return to the LORD your God,
> for he is gracious and compassionate,
> slow to anger and abounding in love,
> and he relents from sending calamity.
> —JOEL 2:13

Adapted from Lisa Bevere, *Out of Control and Loving It!*, 73–79.

INNER BEAUTY TIP

ONLY BY THE SPIRIT

CAN WE LOOK BEYOND

THE OBVIOUS AND

PERCEIVE THE HIDDEN.

You Are Not Whom They See

Do not let your adornment be merely outward...rather let it be the hidden person of the heart, with the incorruptible beauty of a gentle and quiet spirit, which is very precious in the sight of God.

—1 PETER 3:3–4, NKJV

e have talked about unveiling our hearts. Now let's move to the more obvious outward veil of appearances. We are strongly influenced by what we see. Looks can be misleading or deceptive. The outside is not a very reliable indicator of our inward nature. Sometimes the outward even contradicts the inward.

Only by the Spirit can we look beyond the obvious and perceive the hidden. But even those most prophetically anointed find it difficult to do this. Take Samuel, the founding father of the prophetic lineage: He grew up in the temple, ministering to the Lord. God appeared repeatedly to him at Shiloh and clearly revealed Himself by the word of the Lord. This was his reputation:

> The LORD was with him and let none of his words fall to the ground. And all Israel from Dan to Beersheba knew that Samuel had been established as a prophet of the LORD.
> —1 SAMUEL 3:19–20, NKJV

Samuel was so accurate and his heart so pure that God upheld his words. God made sure that not a single one of those words fell to the ground fruitless or unfulfilled. An entire nation recognized God's hand on Samuel's life and honored him as God's mouthpiece. Samuel drew close to God, though he'd been raised up under a corrupt priesthood and disobedient leaders. He knew God's will and accurately discerned God's voice.

Only by the Spirit can we look beyond the obvious and perceive the hidden.

Yet when God sent him to anoint one of Jesse's sons, Samuel was influenced by what he saw. Samuel instructed Jesse to gather his sons.

> When they arrived, Samuel saw Eliab and thought, "Surely the Lord's anointed stands here before the Lord." But the Lord said to Samuel, "Do not consider his appearance or his height, for I have rejected him. The Lord does not look at the things man looks at. Man looks at the outward appearance, but the Lord looks at the heart."
>
> —1 Samuel 16:6–7

A Heart After God

At first, Samuel was certain that Jesse's firstborn, Eliab, was the Lord's anointed. He was impressed by his appearance and stature. Samuel did not see the pride hidden in his heart. In essence, God told

15

Samuel, "Don't be swayed by what you see! Listen to My leading. I see deeper and perceive things you don't." Eliab's appearance had won him the favor of Samuel. But God had another measure or standard—the heart.

God knew man's standard would focus on *the outward appearance.* Whether or not we like it, we are influenced by the appearance of people and things.

> # God knew man's standard would focus on the *outward appearance.*

Let's openly discuss some of the ways the appearance of people may affect us.

The Force of First Impressions

Consider what happens when two professional women are introduced by a mutual friend. Both are young and attractive. They greet each other, extend hands to shake, exchange smiles and make eye contact. Their cordial words do not betray the unspoken discourse going on in their minds.

Woman number one thinks to herself as she makes eye contact: *She is attractive, her hair looks sharp, makeup looks professional. Her lip color is a little bright, but I like her earrings.* Then she lets her eyes drop to scan her hand. *She is single, like me. She is taller, but I'm just as slender. I like her shoes and purse. I wonder what she does for a living?*

Woman number one asks aloud, "What type of business are you in?"

Woman number two has been processing information also. She has determined that woman number one is attractive, that her hair is not its natural color (but she likes it). Woman number one is shorter than she is, even though her heels are higher. She notes that woman number one's legs are not as thin as hers, but she does have a good figure. She likes her suit but would like it better if it were a different color; it washes out her face because her hair color is not natural.

Woman number two answers, "I'm a stockbroker and financial planner. How about you?"

Woman number one is impressed. That is a

high-pressure position. A friendship could be to her advantage since she needs to do some financial planning.

Woman number two asks woman number one to describe her career.

"I'm an attorney with the firm of Lawson and Lawson."

Woman number two nods her respect.

A match has been made. They mutually respect each other professionally, they are both single and self-sufficient, and neither is intimidated by the looks of the other. Their assets and liabilities balance out. They can be friends. Now their conversation will turn toward things that draw them together. Now they can proceed to discuss mutual acquaintances and friends, common hobbies and interests.

Appearance-wise, these hypothetical women were equally matched. But what happens if two very diverse women meet?

WHEN OPPOSITES DON'T ATTRACT

Let's paint a different scenario: A husband and his wife, the mother of his two children, run into his old college friend and the friend's girlfriend at the mall.

The two men are genuinely happy to see each other. They hug and assure each other, "Hey, you look *great!* How are you?"

The husband and father tells his college friend, "George, I want you to meet my wife, Beth. I don't know if you ever met at school. Honey, I knew George my junior year; we had accounting together."

The wife responds, "It's great to meet you, George."

Beth has been uncomfortably eyeing George's girlfriend. She already knows they are not married because she looked for a ring.

"Great to meet you, Beth! I want to introduce Lori to you. Lori, meet Brian and Beth."

"It's nice to meet you," Lori says as she smiles nervously. She feels a little awkward, as if she is on approval. She did not go to school with George, Brian or Beth and is a few years younger than them.

"Nice to meet you, too," Beth answers a little coolly, as her eyes avoid direct contact with Lori's.

The two men begin to catch up as the two

women eye each other awkwardly and scan the mall. Lori is all done up for a date, and Beth is not. Beth doesn't like Lori. Lori is younger and thinner. She is afraid her husband might think George's girlfriend is more attractive than she is. Lori is dressed in a cute shorts outfit. Beth is in a loose and comfortable maternity jumper. She'd put some weight on after her second child. She didn't think they would run into anyone they knew, so she didn't wear makeup. Beth feels self-conscious.

Lori feels awkward in the silence, so she walks over to where Beth is standing off to the side and behind her husband. Before she can make any pleasant conversation, Beth fires off a question:

"How long have you known George?"

"A few years, but we have been dating only for the last few months. How long have you been married?" Lori asks.

"Six years," Beth answers smugly, then adds, "We have two children."

"Wow, that's great!" says Lori.

Beth is intimidated by Lori's warmth and good looks. She does not want to make it easy for her to feel comfortable. She turns from Lori, then reaches out and pulls on her husband's arm. It is her signal that she feels left out and wants to go on with their evening. She doesn't want to ask Lori about Lori. She wants to draw her own conclusions.

"Maybe you and George should go out to lunch sometime so you guys could catch up with each other," Beth suggests, addressing the men and ignoring Lori.

"That would be great!" both men agree. They exchange numbers and promise to call.

The couples part and go in opposite directions.

Later Brian shares with Beth his excitement about running into George and fills her in on George's professional and personal achievements. Beth listens. Then Brian comments on Lori.

"I like Lori; she seems really friendly."

Beth rolls her eyes.

"Why that face?" her husband asks.

"Did you see how tight her top was? She is *friendly*, all right," Beth corrects.

"I didn't notice," Brian answers honestly.

"You know, I had a different figure before I had children," Beth asserts, wanting to disqualify Lori's attractiveness as seductive and transitory while reminding her husband of her own sacrifice. She continues, "If I had all day to spend on my looks and exercise, I could look just as good as Lori! She is probably some airheaded flight attendant!"

Beth is threatened and wants to demean Lori so she can feel better about herself.

Note, the husband only said that Lori was friendly because he had seen her come over to speak to his wife. No mention or comparisons were made about her attractiveness. But Beth is threatened and wants to demean Lori so she can feel better about herself. She wants to lower Lori to a level where she feels that she can compete with her. If Beth can accomplish this, then she will feel safe again.

IT BOILS DOWN TO APPEARANCE

How do I know these types of conversations exist? Because I have carried them on in my mind. I have met women whom I consider different but my equal in appearance and achievement and have embraced them as friends. We can have fun together because we are different enough to be interesting, but not so much as to be intimidating. I have met women I felt were much more attractive and tried to minimize their image because I was intimidated: "John, you do understand that was not her natural hair color."

I have also known the frustration of being judged by my appearance. I have been exasperated when I felt judgment was being passed on me, reducing me to my clothing size. *I hate you! I can't believe you have four children!* This type of greeting is always said in jest…yet you wonder just how much truth is embedded within the humor.

I learned early on the pain of being reduced by what was seen. When I was five, I lost my right eye to cancer. The doctors gave me six months to live. They told my parents I would get a headache, go to sleep and just not wake up. It was a very frightening time for my mother and father, who did not pass this information on to me until much later.

After my eye was removed, I wore a patch

until the swelling was minimized and the socket had healed sufficiently so I could be fitted for an artificial eye.

Before this surgery, everywhere my parents took me, people would stop them and comment, "What a pretty little girl! What beautiful eyes!"

Such compliments always made me uncomfortable when I was young. I was confused because the people looked at *me*, but talked about me to my parents. I would just stand there as my mother or father collected the compliments on my behalf. Then one of my parents would inevitably respond, "What do you say?"

I'd murmur, "Thank you," while dropping my head or looking away.

I didn't care about being called pretty. To me, pretty was almost an insult. I wanted someone to say, "What an incredible tree-climber you have there!" or, "She swims like a fish!"

That was me. *Pretty* was girlish, and I was an avowed *tomboy!* I wanted to be tough and run fast. Pretty meant taking baths, washing your hair, clipping your nails and spending restless nights sleeping in pin curls.

When my eye was removed, the majority of my compliments ceased. Instead, people made strange faces. They studied me from a distance, but still looked a little closer than was comfortable for me.

We lived in a small town, and nearly everyone with whom we had contact knew about my eye. Most studied me with pity, then turned to talk to my mother or father as though I weren't there. Voices would drop to a whisper: "How is she?"

"Fine," my mom would answer aloud.

Then the person would look doubtful and turn to give me a pitying smile, which I answered with a defiant glare. I wanted to yell, "I'm fine. I'm not my eye! I'm not weak; I'm still the same!"

The Cruelty of Judging by Appearance

My surgery took place during the school year. The kids at school called me "one-eye" and "Cyclops." My mother had warned me not to lose face and had told me that name-calling and making fun would only increase if I cried or answered back. She encouraged me to ignore such insults, and she promised me her lap to cry on when I came home from school.

Many days I ran the two miles home from grade school while kids jeered me from the opposite side of the street. I pretended I couldn't hear them and held back my tears until I was home. My mother held me and told me kids this age were cruel, assuring me that when I grew up it would not be like this.

The name-calling did stop, but not the measuring of individuals by outward appearance. We have all grown up, and most of us no longer play the cruel and obvious game of name-calling with our peers. We know that would be blatant judging. But what about more subtle prejudices?

You are not what you see. You are not what they see. So they are not what you see.

The little five-year-old girl in me knew I was not the way I was perceived. At five, I fought against the concept that I could be measured by how I looked, but later in life I embraced this shallow standard.

As children we are not immediately indoctrinated by cultural influences. These forces take some time to mold the metal of our souls. But once the metal is forged, it cools quickly into a hard, rigid standard by which we continually measure ourselves and others.

It is not long before little girls can't wait to be grown-ups. They long to adorn themselves in the outward accessories of makeup and jewelry. They play dress-up and put on cosmetics so they can be their prettiest. Soon they are teens, and they dabble daily in what was once only play. They begin to think they are not pretty without makeup, and what was once reserved for special occasions becomes a daily mandatory ritual. They want to look and act older.

Then something dreadful happens. They finally reach the age they had longed to achieve, and now they are bothered with the worry of getting old. If sixteen to twenty-six is the optimum age range, it is a very short time in the whole scheme of life. As young women approach thirty, they no longer want to look older—they want to look *younger!*

> Once the metal is forged,
> it cools quickly into a hard,
> rigid standard by which
> we continually measure
> ourselves and others.

This is a no-win situation for women. Men don't seem to wrestle with their age quite as much. Their maturing process is more normal. They want to grow up and become independent, but then they don't wig out because they look older! Some women even lie about their age or go to great lengths to hide it. Not content to look great at their real age, they want to appear younger and wiser. Youth and wisdom do not often pair themselves. Wisdom comes with time, obedience and the application of truth. Often we do not have access to these insights until we are old enough to appreciate their importance.

A PRECIOUS ADORNMENT

Young women make the mistake of putting their

trust in their face or form while neglecting their incorruptible assets. We all know the verse in 1 Peter:

> Do not let your adornment be merely out-
> ward—arranging the hair, wearing gold, or
> putting on fine apparel—rather let it be the
> hidden person of the heart, with the incor-
> ruptible beauty of a gentle and quiet spirit,
> which is very precious in the sight of God.
> —1 Peter 3:3–4, NKJV

God admonishes us to not allow our adornment to be merely outward or superficial. He is not telling us not to adorn ourselves, but that the emphasis of our adornment should be on the inside, not the outside. God is not advocating the neglect of our hair, the wearing of rags and the absence of jewelry.

Remember, God's focus is not on the outward appearance; *ours* is. He doesn't judge the way we do. He judges not what is seen, but the unseen condition of the heart. He warns us not to spend ourselves adorning what will not count for eternity. He wants us to adorn our hearts with His unfading, quiet and gentle beauty. It doesn't age, it

29

can't be stolen, and it doesn't turn gray.

> # Young women make the mistake of putting their trust in their face or form while neglecting their incorruptible assets.

Because God's perspective is eternity, He is letting us in on His secret beauty prescription. It is an intimate beauty, one reserved for the eyes of God. It is a kind of beauty others may not notice. But God does.

When you have that inner peace and rest, the world will notice it more than your newest designer outfit, hair color or jewelry. Those in the world have all those things, but what they don't have is peace, "which is of great worth in God's sight" (1 Pet. 3:4).

Those in the world have a confused standard for value and worth. They drape themselves to hide their emptiness while we purify ourselves to gain transparency. They hide while we shine. Unfortunately, we have allowed the marketing of the world's illusions to influence our outward projections and veil our inward reflection.

Judging or Misjudging?

Because we have judged by appearances, we often misjudge. Adornment is like a bowl that holds fruit, one that could be displayed on the dining-room table. It is beautifully crafted and forged of cut crystal, yet holds in its beauty fruit that is artificial and tasteless. The fruit may initially look inviting because it is surrounded by outward beauty, but if handled or sampled, the fruit will soon be revealed as worthless.

Somewhere in the pantry there is a worn and tattered crate that holds real produce. It is not beautiful, yet it bears what is delicious, fresh and life giving. If you were hungry—hungry for truth, hungry for the real—you'd turn from the beauty of the cut crystal bowl filled with artificial fruit and head for the useful, fruitful crate.

God judges us by our *fruit*, not our *fruit bowls*. He wants our inner adornment to be fresh and useful, not cold, beautiful, yet artificial. Therefore, we are mistaken when we judge others by the packaging of outward appearances.

QUESTIONS

Spend a few moments answering the following questions:

How often are you intimidated by what you see outwardly in others?

_____

_____

Have you whittled others down until you are no longer intimidated by them?

_____

_____

What intimidates you the most about other women (weight, beauty, career, marital status, etc.)?

_____

_____

Have you been judged by your appearance?

_____

_____

How was it frustrating to be so judged?

_____

_____

Do you draw your confidence from the outward or the inward?

_____

_____

Which do you spend more time and thought on?

_____

_____

Adapted from Lisa Bevere, *The True Measure of a Woman*, 99–109.

INNER BEAUTY TIP

THE GOAL OF A
FALLEN CULTURE IS
SEXUAL DESIRABILITY
OR ATTRACTIVENESS.

The Image
of the Lie

The fashioners of an image—all of them
are emptiness, and the things they delight
in cannot profit.

—ISAIAH 44:9, RHM

f Jesus is the express image of the truth, then
what is the express image of the lie? Just as
truth needs an image for expression, power
and validation, so the lie must have an image or it
remains powerless.

Actually, we are made painfully and constantly
aware of this image of the lie. It is everywhere we
even happen to glance. It is projected on television
and at the movies, on billboards and splashed

across magazine covers and assorted catalogs. Most of us encounter it daily on one level or another. It is the image built by multitudes of advertising and media experts who feed off our cultural external influences. It is the image of this present culture's ideal woman. In her self, she is nothing; it is what she represents that endangers us.

There are multiple portrayals of her. She is presented to all ethnic groups. She is a woman, perfectly at ease with her self. She moves freely in any setting. She is adored by men and envied by women. All other women are harshly and unfavorably compared with this nameless woman. She never ages; behind her facade of perfection she mocks and makes note of every flaw and imperfection of others.

Her skin is flawless in tone and complexion. Her nose is straight—not too small or too large. Her eyes are bright and lack any dark shadows, circles or lines around them. They are encased in luminous, wrinkle-free skin. Her lips are full and artfully shaped. Her teeth are perfect and gleaming white. Her hair is whatever ours is not.

Her body is perfectly proportioned and sits atop

long, strong legs. Her breasts never age (or nurse)! All too often they are not even real. She is either taller or shorter than we are—the perfect height!

This image is never what we are and is always just beyond our reach, taunting us with her seductive eyes. Who is she anyway?

Her name doesn't really matter; she is not real. She is an image molded and forged by the spirit of this world. What she doesn't have, plastic surgery readily supplies. Even this computer generation will not tolerate any imperfection in her—it reduces her thighs and cinches her waist while sweeping away any sign of imperfection in her skin. She is a deaf, dumb and blind idol.

> This image is never what we are and is always just beyond our reach, taunting us with her seductive eyes.

Though we know she is not real, young girls and older women look at her in awe. The young are inspired, and the older are depressed.

Why would someone we have never met be able to influence us so profoundly? Because we have not allowed the imprint of God to influence us as deeply as she has influenced us. Without a definitive raising of *His* standard, we have accepted the seductive, graven image of the world.

> The fashioners of an image—all of them are emptiness, and the things they delight in cannot profit.
>
> —Isaiah 44:9, rhm

To *fashion* something is to make, model, form or manufacture. In the Bible the words *image* and *idol* are used interchangeably, with the exception of two references. Therefore we could go into the above scripture and bring it forward into today's terms. Then it would read:

> The fashioned idol, modeled idol or fashion image—all of them are empty and lifeless. What they value and prize cannot profit or help you.
>
> —Author paraphrase

Isaiah tells us in the second part of this verse

why this is so: "For their idols neither see nor know. No wonder those who worship them are so ashamed" (TLB). The ancient idols or graven images were forged by craftsmen who made them out of wood or stone. Sometimes they were overlaid with precious metals or costly jewels. But they were never more than lifeless—dead—wood or stone. No matter how dressed up they were on the outside, they had no life on the inside.

The people would model and form images and idols and then bow down to what they themselves had crafted. These crafted images (of wood, stone, or precious metals) were made by the created (humans). Then the created subjected themselves to the crafted. Crying out to images without breath, those with eyes asked guidance of blind idols. Those with breath, mouth and voice cried out to mute idols with lifeless lips. Those with ears to hear cried out to deaf ears of stone. They offered fragrant incense and food to idols who could neither smell nor taste.

The created longed to worship the work of their own hands, though these idols could never raise a finger in response. The created cannot *create*—it can only *craft*. The crafted cannot even craft.

When we worship the works
of our hands or the works of
the flesh, we are worshiping
images of the *creation* and
not the Creator.

It all seems rather silly to us. Most of us would never bow our knees to an idol or seek wisdom from a graven image. So what does this have to do with us?

When we worship the works of our hands or the works of the flesh, we are worshiping images of the *creation* and not the Creator. Let's go into the New Testament to find how this could be relevant today:

> For although they knew God, they neither glorified him as God nor gave thanks to him, but their thinking became futile and their foolish hearts were darkened.
>
> —Romans 1:21

They knew there was a Creator God, but they did not want to glorify Him or acknowledge His provision by thanking Him. They turned their eyes from God and began to worship images. Soon their hearts became like the idols they worshiped—void of light and futile. This parallels Isaiah's description of useless idols.

The image you behold is the image you become—not outwardly but inwardly.

The concept is further expanded by Paul the Apostle in the Book of Romans:

> Although they claimed to be wise, they became fools and exchanged the glory of the immortal God for images made to look like mortal man and birds and animals and reptiles.
>
> —Romans 1:22–23

The idol worshipers claimed to be wise creators, but when you bow to that which is equal (mere man) or lower than your self, you become degraded, abased and deceived. When you serve what is lifeless you die.

Therefore God gave them over in the sinful

desires of their hearts to sexual impurity for the degrading of their bodies with one another. *They exchanged the truth of God for a lie,* and worshiped and served created things rather than the Creator—who is forever praised. Amen.
—ROMANS 1:24–25, EMPHASIS ADDED

They wanted to serve the works of their flesh, so God let them become mastered by their flesh. They worshiped images fashioned after their own desires, so God turned them over to their basest of desires. Where there is idol or image worship, we always find sexual sin. It comes in the form of promiscuity and perversion. Sexual impurity is accompanied by an increased prominence of sexual expression. Nudity is common. What once was saved for intimacy is now displayed for all to view. Men and women who were inwardly fashioned for the habitation of the Spirit of God instead become temples of sexual perversion and depravity.

Sexual suggestion is used to sell everything in our current culture. The goal of a fallen culture is sexual desirability or attractiveness. You can study any fallen ancient culture and find this to be true.

In today's culture, those who are not viewed as sexually desirable are not assigned much worth. The undesirables are the older, the overweight and the out of shape.

We exchange the truth for a lie whenever we worship or serve the created and not the Creator.

If you are afraid of being sexually abused, you will often hide your self within walls of excess flesh or starve your self in an attempt to return to your childhood. To our culture, sexual perversion or promiscuity is merely physical. Unfortunately, this physical-body mentality has even crept into the church. Yet we know there is a much deeper and stronger spiritual connection tying the physical/sexual realm to the unseen spiritual/worship realm.

We exchange the truth for a lie whenever we worship or serve the created and not the Creator.

Before we go further it is important to describe the worship of idols or idolatry in contemporary terms. Until we do so, idolatry still may seem a foreign term. An *idol* is anything you draw your strength from or give your strength to. It is how you spend your self—your time, your efforts, your thoughts. It is the driving force behind your actions. It is what makes you feel confident and comfortable. *Nelson's Illustrated Bible Dictionary* defines an *idol* as "something we ourselves make into a god." It can be anything that stands between us and God—a substitute for God.

As Christians it is important to determine whether we are serving an image of God or God Himself. There are three options:

- Unwittingly we may fashion or mold our own image to serve.
- We may bow to the one our culture readily provides.
- We may cry out to God and ask Him to reveal Himself (and in response, we worship Him).

Our image of God is an image that will service

44

our *selves*. It is the god of *me*. It is the result of trying to conform God to our image. He may be a hard taskmaster or a "sugar daddy," based on our unique and individual frame of reference. But this image or idol is a mere spectre of the real. It is limited to our own past experiences and perceptions. It is forged in the realm of our reasoning, and we know that God sees things completely differently than we do (Isa. 55:8–9).

If we are serving the gods or idols of this world, we will recognize this in our desire to conform to the world's image. We will want the acceptance and approval of our culture. We will desire what our culture desires. We will seek its reward and system of social and financial security. The image will always be before us, inviting and enticing us to be like it. We will look toward it, gauging our success or failures according to the messages we receive from these idols.

God is calling us to radical transformation.

If we are serving God and not merely an image from any other source, we will experience a constant and ongoing transformation into His image. All lasting liberation, healing or change begins with inward transformation.

If we are truthful, we will admit to visiting all three temples: the god of flesh, the god of soul and the God of spirit.

God is calling us to radical transformation. You've known the lie; you've been introduced to the truth. Now it is time to be honest. What image are you serving?

Have you cried out to fashioned idols and images, longing to be conformed to their shape, size or image? Did you think they would bring you love and happiness? Perhaps you have thought that transformation would be too difficult for God to accomplish in your life, so you've continued to struggle in your own strength.

It's time for you to repent of reducing the image of God to your own level of understanding, reasoning, knowledge, ability or experience. By repenting, you renounce the hold and influence of the idols in your life. This will be an act of submission to God and aggression against a long-term spiritual stronghold in our culture.

Allow God to reveal Himself to you in a deeper and very real way. Give him permission to invade this private and personal area of your life. He sees beyond what you see—and in His strength you will learn to see yourself through His eyes.

Adapted from *You Are Not What You Weigh*, 29–35.

INNER BEAUTY TIP

SELF IMAGE IS A
DEFENSIVE MECHANISM.
IT IS THE IMAGE WE PROJECT
WHILE WE TRY TO PROTECT
WHO WE REALLY ARE.

4

The Image of Self

He must become greater; I must become less.

—JOHN 3:30

In the last chapter we introduced the image, or idol, of the lie. There is yet another area of "image worship" that needs to be confronted in our process to freedom. We have been imprisoned by deceptive lords—ones who tricked us into allegiance and then threw us into dungeons and prisons when we didn't meet their incessant demands. Through repentance we are removed out from under their legal jurisdiction and freed to live under the authority and protection promised in the kingdom of God.

> He has rescued us from the dominion of
> darkness and brought us into the kingdom
> of the Son he loves.
>
> —COLOSSIANS 1:13

All forms of captivity are under the authority and dominion of darkness. By renouncing our allegiance to their cause and wholeheartedly asking the Lord to forgive any sympathy or inclination toward their domain, the power of His Son is there to rescue us from the images that have held us captive. Having renounced any tendency toward the image of the world, it is now time to go a step further and renounce another prevalent image.

This image is much more subtle and widely accepted in most religious circles, though it is not found on any list in the kingdom. It actually is a religious idea, one of the very first to be introduced. Yet, there is a problem with religious ideas and traditions: They are powerless to liberate us. Jesus explained it this way:

> You have let go of the commands of God

and are holding on to the traditions of men
…setting aside the commands of God in
order to observe your own traditions…
Thus you nullify the word of God by your
tradition that you have handed down.

—Mark 7:8–9, 13

It is yet another example of turning away from
the living commands of God to conform to the
wisdom and traditions of man—an example of
turning from the Creator toward the created. Jesus
explained that in so doing, they nullified—
negated or canceled out—the very power they
needed. Power is not found in principles but hidden within the Word of God. The religious people
of Jesus' day exchanged the truth for a lie, life for
death and power for impotence.

Power is not found in principles but hidden within the Word of God.

We need the Word of God, for hidden in its

manifold truths is the power of God. Though the word of man may contain form and structure, without the life and power of God it is useless. It cannot transform our hearts though it may please our heads. We need substance and relationship. To apprehend this we must strip away yet another veil, the veil of self worship.

You may immediately reject this, arguing, "How could I worship my self? I feel bad about my self. I have a bad self image!"

> God does not want us fulfilled through the avenue of self. He wants us fulfilled through Him.

To this objection I would counter, "Whenever you are limited to your self image, then the image *of* self becomes your master."

At this time I want to challenge some typical deceptions. Here is one: If only I could feel good about my self, then I would be fulfilled.

God does not want us fulfilled through the avenue of self. He wants us fulfilled through Him. The Word of God is not set up to cause us to feel good about our selves. It is set up to reveal to us a good God. To feel good about our selves, we have to be good. But even Jesus would not assign the adjective of *good* to Himself.

> "Why do you call me good?" Jesus answered. "No one is good—except God alone."
>
> —MARK 10:18; CF. LUKE 18:19

Notice He did not say, "Wow, God must have told you that! Thanks, I really feel encouraged and much better about My self. I am good, and you can be good, too! Just follow Me!"

No, His answer to the rich young ruler was of a very different sort. He wasn't looking to be labeled as "good" by human standards; His goal was to glorify His heavenly Father, who is the very essence of goodness.

Though Jesus was the Son of God, He did not grasp at equality with God the Father by calling Himself good. God alone is good, and through His goodness we are restored and He is glorified.

I want to address self image first on a personal level and then on a spiritual level. An image of self is not something we are born with; it is forged through pain, pressure and praise.

Pain will cause us to become aware of something of which we previously were not aware. When I had my first son, the delivery left me with back problems. Until then I never even noticed my back. Now, pain brought it to the forefront.

Pressure will bring hidden or under-the-surface talents or flaws to the surface. Competition is set up with pressures to pit one against another in a setting where the talents and abilities of one will contrast with the others. A child might think he is the fastest runner in his class, but until race day it is not known.

Praise will test what you are made of and point out talents or assets. The Bible tells us a person is tested by the praise he receives (Prov. 27:21). One of my children received a lot of attention for his hair. It was something he couldn't care less about, but it constantly set him apart when he received comments like, "Your children are handsome—

especially this one. Look at his hair!" Being a boy, these comments bothered him, and we eventually cut his hair. But a girl might have been tempted to draw her self worth from such compliments.

These processes cause us to become aware or conscious of our selves, or self conscious. A collective number of common occurrences raise our level of awareness of what was previously not apparent to us.

For example, at age three, my youngest son was beautiful, yet totally unaware of the concept of beauty. This unawareness made him that much more attractive. His goal was not to be attractive, but to be expressive. His objective was to give love and receive love. At three years of age, he didn't even know the color of his eyes. However, he knew—and still knows—that he was loved, cared for and to whom he belonged; those things were enough for him. He was free!

I saw it in the pictures he drew and heard it in the animated tone of his voice. He liked to hold my face between his two soft hands and look at me face to face. He wanted me up close in order to know he had my full attention and affection. He looked me intently in the eyes until I returned his gaze; then he kissed me. He needed the closeness. In it, he was not aware of his self—he was only aware of the two of us.

This is what God wants for us—that we might be so totally aware of our relationship with Him that we lose consciousness of what is around us. He doesn't want to draw us close to see our flaws; He wants to hold us close to captivate us with His love.

> This is what God wants for us—that we might be so totally aware of our relationship with Him that we lose consciousness of what is around us.

A few years ago I had a vivid dream in which the Lord spoke passionately to me in that twilight before waking: "Don't just glance at Me; I want you to behold Me. I want you held captive by My gaze."

I realized He was asking for a new level of intensity in our relationship. I saw my self glance over to Him for guidance, direction or protection—looking, then turning away, looking, then turning back to what was in front of me. When I heard His call to behold Him, my gaze became fixed upon Him.

When John and I were first engaged, we could be in a room full of other women and men and yet see only each other. If I left the room, I'd return to find him watching for me. His eyes would light up when he saw me. Our eyes would lock, and that would be it. Unless we were interrupted, no one else existed for us. I wasn't aware of my self; I was only aware of *us*. It was no longer "John and Lisa"; it was an awareness that the two of us were one.

Each of us began life with this same unawareness of self, but when did it leave? This usually happens progressively as we are exposed to the opinions of others and when we allow those opinions to influence us more than the opinions of God.

Somewhere between childhood and adulthood we lose our bearings. Whether we intended to or not, we exchanged the truth for a lie. We began to believe we are what we do, what we have, what we wear, what we know, how we look, whom we know and what we weigh.

I remember acutely being thrust into this arena of self consciousness, very much against my own will. When I lost my right eye to cancer, it meant going to school with a patch over my eye until the swelling went down and the eye socket was ready to be fitted with a prosthesis. I remember beginning kindergarten as a normal child and two weeks later returning as a freak. I was intensely aware of the stares and jests of my peers. It was more obvious than the gauze adhesive bandage on my face. The bandage no longer seemed to cover merely my eye. Now my very soul felt entangled and entrapped in that gauze bandage.

I no longer felt free of my self. I felt restrained by it. I began to scan the faces of others to see how I should feel about my self. If they were repulsed, then it meant I must be repulsive. I didn't question their assessment. My first-grade picture shows a very different girl from the one found in my kindergarten photo taken before my eye was removed. There had been more than an eye loss; there had also been a loss of innocence. I had lost a great measure of my self unawareness, and with it I had lost my confidence. Before I lost my eye, my confidence was not placed in how I looked. I had been unaware of my looks. I had been free. Now I was bound to my looks as surely as a prisoner bound by chains.

For each of us it happens in different measures and at various times. Whenever there is diversity or differences, we find comparisons and criticism. Most of us remember the agony we all endured during the various stages of puberty. That's when I remember being most body conscious. I felt as though my body had betrayed me.

I was a very late bloomer, and I decided I didn't want to bloom at all. I came to this conclusion after hearing from my peers who had gone before me and from watching various health movies on what I would have to endure. I did not want bra straps for boys to snap. I had no desire to shave my legs and underarms. The very thought of bleeding and cramping monthly sounded like a horrible intrusion on my favorite sport—swimming. (Even now it still does.)

Each girl was assessed according to her physical

development. Boys noticed the girls who were developing quickly. Gone were the days of equal chest size. For me the word *flat* took on a totally new meaning. I learned the art of creative draping during PE class as I tried to maintain a delicate balance between getting in and out of my gym suit and my clothes. I was beginning to feel a further separation between the physical me and the real me…the obvious and the unseen.

> To lose consciousness
> of one's self happens
> when we become more
> conscious or aware of
> God and His will than we
> are of self and its will.

As children, our bodies served us, but it was not long before we found our selves serving them. Perhaps you were an early bloomer. You were made aware of your physical side in a positive light. But still you were reduced to something temporal and subject to change. People praised the obvious while missing the unseen. So you developed the obvious and neglected the unseen.

Self image is a defense mechanism. It is the image we project while we try to protect who we really are. It's the projected image versus the protected one. Self image is the one left vulnerable when we lose the innocence of self unawareness. In a moment's time, most of us lose the unconscious sense of our physical body. In that instant we became tethered to what has now become awkward and uncomfortable.

The opposite of self conscious is not a "good" self image or self esteem. The opposite of *conscious* is *unconscious*. To lose consciousness of one's self happens when we become more conscious or aware of God and His will than we are of self and its will. This is a work of the Spirit, accomplished progressively as we renounce our natural limitations and abandon our selves to Him.

Adapted from *You Are Not What You Weigh*, 43–50.

INNER BEAUTY TIP

IN CHRIST OUR FOCUS IS
RESTORED AGAIN TO THE
ETERNAL. BY LOSING SIGHT
OF THE SEEN WE GAIN
THE UNSEEN.

5

God's Definition

You are a chosen people, a royal priesthood, a holy nation, a people belonging to
God, that you may declare the praises of
him who called you out of darkness into
his wonderful light.

—1 PETER 2:9

ho defines a woman? What defines her? We already know we cannot trust the definition of our culture, since it defines women in terms of the physical. The goal of a fallen culture is to be sexually attractive because it is emblazoned with lust. (See Romans 1:26–27.)

Though it begins with apparent innocence, young girls become enmeshed in the fantasy of growing up to be beautiful and desirable. After all, nearly every childhood movie alleges that it is the young and beautiful who marry and find happiness. Yet we've grown up and discovered that attractiveness is not enough to hold a family together. This dream rings hollow in our culture, with more than half of all marriages ending in divorce.

> From the very beginning God created woman to support, to complete— not to compete.

When the world's fantasy of the perfect family didn't work, our culture re-created its image of the ideal woman, in turn redefining the family. Society encouraged women to leave behind their bondage of servitude. Women were urged to become the master of their own destiny. The new image claimed that motherhood is boring—why waste your time on children when you can have a career? Stay-at-home mothers were despised as weak and lazy; the image of the independent career woman was embraced. Why not have it all! As the image demoralized, love was replaced with lust—a lust for power, security and control. The image of a desirable woman changed from gentle, faithful and maternal to free-spirited, self-willed and wanton. From a nurturer to a controller.

Yet from the very beginning God created woman to support, to complete—not to compete. This is the case whether a woman is married or single. Women are nurturers by nature, and this strength can be translated to the professional as well as personal. Whether a woman is a single doctor or a stay-at-home mother, she can still bring the nature of a servant to any level. Not simply because she is a woman but because she is a Christian. We have a genderless command to:

> Above all, love each other deeply, because love covers over a multitude of sins…Each one should use whatever gift he has received to serve others, faithfully administering God's grace in its various forms.
>
> —1 PETER 4:8–10

Independent of our marital, professional or social status, our talents and abilities are not to be used to serve our *selves,* but to serve *others.* We each have an opportunity to serve God in our unique sphere of influence. God plants each of us in various soils to accomplish His purpose.

The world is preaching an opposing gospel. Almost without exception the covers of secular women's magazines boast young, seductive women and promise to reveal the secrets to great sex, ageless beauty and thinner thighs. All of these are meant to entice subscribers with self gratification. They offer slavery to the lust of this world while God offers servitude. Their message: Live for the moment; live for pleasure; live for your self!

> # God plants each of us in various soils to accomplish His purpose.

But what is the message of Christ? How can those of us who know the truth help spread the truth?

Letting go of lies can be frightening until truth is revealed. In obedience we renounced the lie and its idolatry; now we need to glean the precious from the vile. Most of us were led astray because we were looking—no, longing—for someone to define us.

I remember my freshman year in college. I found myself with more options than direction. In high school, classes are scheduled to accomplish the goal of graduation and not to focus on any specific area of study. I'd run away out west, far from all that was familiar; then I lost my bearings. Removed from my usual frame of reference, I felt vulnerable and confused. I wanted to dream yet didn't dare fail.

I wanted to study premed, but I feared I wasn't smart enough. I had scored high on the required ACT exam but only modestly on the SAT exam. I wasn't certain if I was smart, stupid or somewhere in between. During the first semester I went to the university guidance counselor and shared my dilemma. I requested additional testing in order to determine first if I was smart enough and second, if I had the aptitude.

When test day came I was a nervous wreck. I felt as though my whole future hung in the balance. It was a week or so before the results would be available. When I returned for the interpretation of the results, I was disappointed. My aptitudes ranged from dean of women to a podiatrist. My IQ results were inconclusive as well. "You're creative and excel at math and science. You are smart enough to be whatever you choose," the guidance counselor assured me.

"Are you certain?" I questioned.

"Yes. As long as you apply yourself, you can do anything," she answered.

This was not what I wanted to hear. I wanted precise and specific direction in order to apply myself. I wanted her to say something like this: "These test results show without a doubt that you can be a doctor in this field of medicine."

I questioned her further. "But what if I don't apply myself? Will I still succeed?"

Of course this question was stupid, and I'm sure at that moment she questioned the test results herself, for she glanced again at the folder in her hand. With a perplexed look she assured me that if I did *not* apply myself I would *not* be successful. As I left I thought, *I am not smart enough. I will not even try if there is a chance I might fail. I will choose another area of study.*

What did I want from her? I wanted her to define me. I wanted her to remove all the self doubt that clouded my mind. I wanted clear directions to eliminate all chances for failure. I wanted a guarantee. I wanted her to tell me who I was and what I could and could not do. By taking the test I wanted conclusive direction. When I did not get this, I floated through college aimlessly. I wanted the test to tell me what I myself doubted. I wanted her professional faith in me to overcome my insecurities and fears. I could believe in the test, I could believe in her, but I found it difficult to believe in my self.

I continued my search elsewhere. At that stage in my life I received a lot attention from guys—perhaps one of them would define me. I moved in and out of relationships trying to find a fit. I chose guys who were hard to please and tried to be whatever they saw in me. I was like a chameleon. If they wanted me to be intelligent, I pursued academics. If they found me attractive, I was seductive. But it was always just a matter of time before I grew discontented. As soon as they molded or labeled me,

I became uncomfortable and broke off the relationship. I realized their perceptions were inaccurate because I was living a lie by pretending to be someone I was not.

I had been pretending for a long time. At first it had been easy. There was the pretend me and the real me, the projected image and the protected one. But it was not long before the distinctions began to blur. The projected me was so busy trying to win approval and give the appearance of strength that I soon forgot who I really was, who it was I was protecting. As this progressed, I didn't like being alone. I wanted to be in a constant social setting. If you couldn't show me a good time, I didn't want to be around you. I was shallow and thoughtless. I was nothing more than what you saw. I was what I weighed, what I wore, whom I dated. Like so many, I had conformed to the cultural image and felt empty and lost.

My own fear of failure and desire for approval from men drove me to live such a lie. I chose to allow those around me to define me. I conformed to a lie. I could blame my father, boyfriends, a painful past or brazen cultural influences, but the truth is, I had been void of truth, so I embraced lies.

Until I met Jesus, the Truth was not in me. I had to spurn the man-made information to embrace transformation. Transformation could only come by renewing my mind, by reading His Word. This meant I had to leave behind my former ways.

> You've been untethered
> from the lie; now I want
> you bound to truth.

You may have been already acquainted with Jesus when you began this book. But in this area of image, perhaps you were more acquainted with the message of the world than the message of Christ. I believe that as you have read, you've recognized and repented of these sympathies. This has released and empowered you to walk in truth. It is my prayer that you would never be entangled again. You've been untethered from the lie; now I want you bound to truth.

Jesus is that truth. As we live and apply His

truth, we will walk on the path of ever-increasing light.

> The path of the righteous is like the first gleam of dawn, shining ever brighter till the full light of day.
>
> —Proverbs 4:18

The prayers and steps you've taken in good faith have placed your feet on the path of righteousness. At the first gleam of dawn the light is dim, but as we continue toward the light of His Word it grows brighter. The psalmist said, "Your word is a lamp to my feet and a light to my path" (Ps. 119:105, NKJV). Our understanding is illuminated as we read His Word. It is important to approach the Word with humility. There is danger when we go to the Word to gather information to establish our opinions or beliefs. We then read what we believe, instead of believing what we read. When we go to the Word with a teachable, meek and humble heart we are transformed. Dim eyes are flooded with the light of spiritual wisdom and understanding for the revelation of God.

I pray that your hearts will be flooded with

> light so that you can understand the won-
> derful future he has promised to those he
> called. I want you to realize what a rich and
> glorious inheritance he has given to his
> people.
>
> —EPHESIANS 1:18, NLT

In Christ is embodied every dream and hope,
not only in heaven but as an inheritance for us on
earth. He gives us purpose, plans and a future. His
death defines our life.

> Set your minds on things above, not on
> earthly things. For you died, and your life is
> now hidden with Christ in God. When
> Christ, who is your life, appears, then you
> also will appear with him in glory.
>
> —COLOSSIANS 3:2–4

He is our life. He is "Christ in you, the hope of
glory" (Col. 1:27). Because our lives are hidden in
Him, our mind, desires and affections should be
set on things above, not on earthly things. When
Adam and Eve were in the garden, their minds
went from the heavenly and eternal to the earthly
and temporal. In Christ our focus is restored again

to the eternal. By losing sight of the seen we gain the unseen. At the revelation of God's glory we will be seen for what we really are.

Because our lives are hidden
in Him, our mind, desires
and affections should be
set on things above,
not on earthly things.

Paul continues his letter to explain this transformation:

> …since you have put off the old man with his deeds, and have put on the new man who is renewed in knowledge according to the image of Him who created him.
>
> —Colossians 3:9–10, NKJV

At the time of our rebirth we put on a new man (or woman) who is being renewed or regenerated inwardly until it takes on the image of its Creator. We will be restored to the original image God intended for us. No longer will we be formed in the image of man; we are once again created in the image of God.

Looking at ourselves we see the possible; looking at God we see the impossible.

When I look at God's holiness, then look at myself, it seems impossible that I have been created in the image of God! Looking at ourselves we see the possible; looking at God we see the impossible. What is impossible with man is possible with God. We are not to measure what God can do with and through us by what we have done. We are not the focus; the possibility of our new image is not based on us—but on a victory Christ has already won. It does not matter how many times you may have tried and failed; it is not about you or your ability.

Do not be afraid; you will not suffer shame.
Do not fear disgrace; you will not be

humiliated.
You *will forget* the shame of your youth
and remember no more the reproach of
your widowhood.
—Isaiah 54:4, emphasis added

This is God's promise. An invitation to leave behind our prison of fear. He assures us that shame and humiliation will not be our future, and He promises to erase all the shameful memories and reproach of our past. This promise is available to each child of God. It is for those who will dare to believe and thereby mix His precious words with faith. Your past is not your future! He holds out the hope of a future free from the fear of failure. In the Book of Philippians Paul shared his feelings of imperfection, and then he gave us the key to his walk with God:

Forgetting what is behind and straining toward what is ahead…
—Philippians 3:13

When we look to our past we forsake our future. When the woman taken in adultery was brought before Jesus, He told her, "Go and sin no more" (John 8:11, NKJV). Notice He did not say, "I know you have a problem with men because you never had a healthy relationship with your father. I want you to go through six months of counseling, and once you have figured this all out then you will be able to go and sin no more." Her past did not matter; His forgiveness and word held the power to free her. Looking again to the past arouses doubt and reawakens our self consciousness, thus reducing our God consciousness.

> Because Jesus thought
> you were something
> worth dying for,
> you can be truly alive.

You may say, "It is all too simple." Human nature is often drawn to the difficult and complex, but I find God most often in the pure and simple. You are free. The light has shone on your path. Now the choice is yours. Will you walk in the light?

Until God imparted His purpose and plan into

my life, I felt entirely purposeless. Our purpose or calling defines us. He defined us with His death:

> You are a chosen people, a royal priest-hood, a holy nation, a people belonging to God, that you may declare the praises of him who called you out of darkness into his wonderful light.
>
> —1 Peter 2:9

God defines us because He has chosen us. He separated us from the world to bring us back to Himself. He delivered us out darkness into the light so that we would declare His praises. We belong to Him, purchased by the priceless blood of His Son.

Because Jesus thought you were something worth dying for, you can be truly alive. He exchanged His vibrant, abundant life for your gray and lifeless one.

By whose definition will you live?

Adapted from *You Are Not What You Weigh,* 151–160.

Conclusion

God does not want our money or labor—He wants our empty lives. In exchange for our surrender, He gives us life, an everlasting covenant and faithful, unwavering love. He fills our lives with His beauty so we can radiate His glory through our lives.

But we cannot come to Him in the strength of our own merits. We must strip our selves from the lies and embrace His truth. He is calling us to the river of baptism, where we are totally immersed into life and all that is death is washed away. Such a rebirth is available in every area of our lives.

We must look beyond what we see to what He sees.

We must look beyond what we see to what He sees. We must acknowledge our need for Him, our need for His help. We must ask Him to sow a seed of truth into the soil of our humbled heart. This seed is found in His Word.

> As the rain and the snow
> come down from heaven,
> and do not return to it
> without watering the earth
> and making it bud and flourish,
> so that it yields seed for the sower and
> bread for the eater,
> so is my word that goes out from my mouth:
> It will not return to me empty,
> but will accomplish what I desire
> and achieve the purpose for which I sent
> it.
> —Isaiah 55:10–11

The seed of truth is first planted in the rich soil of your spirit. Guarded there, it is allowed a safe atmosphere in which to grow. As it grows, we must tend it as we would a natural garden, watering it with the truth of God's Word and uprooting any additional weeds of destruction and deception.

Some of the seeds that have been planted in your life may have been seeds that produced pain or destruction. Such seeds need to be uprooted. New seeds of truth should be planted—ones that will yield a harvest of healing and strength for your life.

Are you ready to radiate with the inner beauty of a life filled with God's image?

Are you ready to allow the Master Gardener to transform you? Are you ready to radiate with the inner beauty of a life filled with God's image? Allow God to make you beautiful in Him.

Adapted from *You Are Not What You Weigh*, 21–23.

If you are enjoying the Inner Beauty Series by Lisa Bevere, here are some other titles from Charisma House that we think will minister to you…

Out of Control and Loving It!
Lisa Bevere
ISBN: 0-88419-436-1
Retail Price: $12.99

Lisa Bevere's life was a whirlwind of turmoil until she discovered that whenever she was in charge, things ended up in a mess. *Out of Control and Loving It!* is her journey from fearful, frantic control to a haven of rest and peace under God's control.

You Are Not What You Weigh
Lisa Bevere
ISBN: 0-88419-661-5
Retail Price: $10.99

Are you tired of reading trendy diet books, taking faddish pills and ordering the latest in infomercial exercise equipment? This is not another "how-to-lose-weight" book. Dare to believe, and this will be the last book you'll need to finally end your war with food and break free from the bondage of weight watching.

The True Measure of a Woman
Lisa Bevere
ISBN: 0-88419-487-6
Retail Price: $11.99

In her frank, yet gentle manner, Lisa Bevere exposes the subtle influences and blatant lies that hold many women captive. With the unveiling truth of God's Word, she displaces these lies and helps you discover who you are in Christ.

 To pick up a copy of any of these titles, contact your local Christian bookstore or order online at www.charismawarehouse.com.